abide

REST IN THE RUNNING

Come to me, all who labor and are heavy laden,
and I will give you **rest**.
Take my yoke upon you, and learn from me,
for I am gentle and lowly in heart,
and you will find **rest** for your souls.

- Matthew 11:28-29

With gratitude to the contributing authors, who each retain the copyright for their individual works.

ISBN 978-1-7360844-2-7

Published by Copperlight Wood
P.O. Box 870697
Wasilla, AK
99687
www.copperlightwood.com

Design and photography by Shannon Guerra, excepting page 56 by Megan Ancheta.

Portions of scripture in **bold** are the author's emphasis.

This title may be purchased in bulk for ministry or group study use. For more information, please email shop@copperlightwood.com.

Printed and bound in the USA.

contributors

MĒGAN ANCHETA

homeschool mom, yarn snob,
owner of Allergy Free Alaska, LLC
www.allergyfreealaska.com
allergyfreealaska@gmail.com

JESSICA DASSOW

wrangler of many boys and a princess,
drinker of unintentionally cold tea,
certified childbirth educator
www.planted-by-the-river.com

CYNTHIA HELLMAN

bibliophile, desert dweller,
homeschooling mom, theatre nerd
www.cultivatedgraftings.blogspot.com

NATASHA METZLER

author, adoptive mom, farm life chronicler,
believer in miracles
www.natashametzler.com
natashametzler@gmail.com

RENEE PETTY

wife, boy mom, lover of Jesus,
third generation Alaskan, pursuer of healing,
Christmas fanatic, champion of freedom

contents

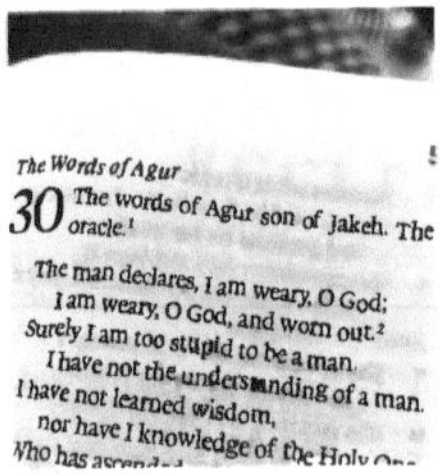
The Words of Agur
30 The words of Agur son of Jakeh. The oracle.
The man declares, I am weary, O God;
I am weary, O God, and worn out.
Surely I am too stupid to be a man.
I have not the understanding of a man.
I have not learned wisdom,
nor have I knowledge of the Holy One

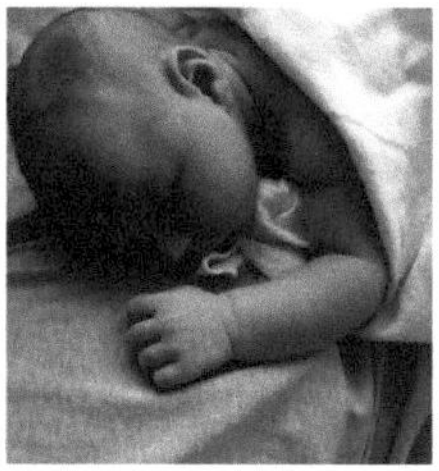

And when they had entered, they went up to **the upper room**, where they were staying... All these with one accord were **devoting themselves to prayer**, together with the women and Mary the mother of Jesus, and his brothers.

- ACTS 1:13-14

It is a new year again

and we are an

upper room people:

expectant, alert,

watchful, waiting.

The colors are coming

together in a glorious

and beautiful way.

upper room people

Every time the new year rolls around, someone needs to hear this, and surely it's not just me:

This year is a clean slate, yes, but it's meant to be written on.

Things will get smudgy. And if your year already has a smear or two on it, it doesn't mean you've ruined anything. Like a brand new house getting its first scratch or ding, it just means you've been living in it. There's no pressure to keep things sterile and perfect, Love – tomorrow is always new day.

Some of these days will seem like nothing special, full of repetition and fits and starts. Here's an example of one of mine: I write emails. I edit my husband's next post. I package books. I attempt journaling three times but am thwarted by our baby, who wakes up from his nap every. single. time. And I help our toddler latch the lid on a huge leftover container that he has picked out, now holding fifteen calories worth of cheese that he simply could not finish for lunch.

But the most important thing I'll do all day? I'll pray. It's the thing that lasts, that changes tomorrow, that allows the Lord to rearrange and realign our thoughts. It's what continually cleans the smears off our hearts and our days.

I pray for my kids and my husband. I pray for my readers. I pray for the people driving on the road, and for the traffic on the highway. I pray for friends and situations that the Lord brings to mind. And I pray for people who annoy me on Facebook (not you, of course).

I don't pray because I'm so great; I pray because He is. I pray because we need Him to come into our homes and hearts and cities and bodies, so He can do the editing in the stories we write.

And we need His editing because our stories are ridiculous.

Maybe like you, I am the exhausted mom of many who, on laundry day, asks the kids to unbury the couch only to be met with vehement protests like, "Why? No one's coming over." I am the mom who wonders why we cook meals for our children when they're totally happy with raw biscuit dough and frozen peas straight from the bag. I am the mom who googled "how to clean crayon from laundry and dryer" and considered a complete embargo on all things blue Crayola. (I also considered ice cream for dinner and an early bedtime.)

And the Lord, who wants to be found and known, is with us in these ridiculous, bright colored days. He doesn't play games and tricks, hiding like a leprechaun. He is near, watching, loving, waiting to be seen as He watches us, and moving in us to make us more like Him.

Seek the Lord while he may be found;
call upon him while he is near;
let the wicked forsake his way,
and the unrighteous man his thoughts;
let him return to the Lord, that he may have compassion on him,
and to our God, for he will abundantly pardon.
For my thoughts are not your thoughts,
neither are your ways my ways, declares the Lord.
For as the heavens are higher than the earth,
so are my ways higher than your ways
and my thoughts than your thoughts.
– *Isaiah* 55:6-9

This abiding with Him is rest, not striving. Not stressing, not impressing, not trying to prove ourselves. It is loving the place we're in, because He is the place we're in. It is looking to Him as the shelter, and not the physical stuff or circumstances around us.

The real miracle is that when we abide in Him, He abides right back in us - He makes us His home, and starts rearranging everything in the best way.

But sometimes that's a new thing for us to get used to, because we tend to like doing our own rearranging. Yet this same God who sees and knows and wants to be known also tells us, "It is not for you to know the times or seasons ...But you will receive power when the Holy Spirit has come upon you..." [1]

And I am a planner, a strategizer who likes to know the times and seasons.

I want to know the details and prepare for contingencies and possibilities. But Jesus asks us, "Do you want the plan? Or do you want the power?" And when you put it that way, well, duh – I want the power. Especially since it's something He wants to give me.

We often settle for less because we're fighting fear and anxiety of the unknown, and we want control. But control is not power; surrender and faith are power. And He brings those as we abide.

So on these new days in this new year, we'll do a bunch of things. We'll make meals and messes. We will write things on the calendar and cross them out. We'll make our plans while yielding to Him, resting in all the mundane and ridiculous and glorious moments as He shows us how to pray.

But we'll find Him in deep pockets of rest, letting Him teach us to hold the balance we long for in perfect tension. It's how we'll refill after we empty ourselves out, over and over, instead of trying to manufacture fresh water from the muddy dregs at the bottom of an overused well – because He is the Living Water, and we are the upper room people abiding in Him.

what we need for now

I never used to be a bath person. I mean, it was *nice*...a giant soaker tub in your master bathroom is nothing to shake a stick at. But it took me almost nine years to truly appreciate our tub on a regular basis, when it became a Wednesday night tradition to compensate for Wednesday morning madness on our craziest day of the week.

I just didn't realize how badly I needed it. And when I did, it became the refuge and refilling I looked forward to all week: a stack of books, a hot bath, and a quiet room with no one else in it. I could shut the door on the world of chaos downstairs while my husband did dinner and bedtime with the kids.

But one day I was in Exodus, reading the Ten Commandments for the bazillionth time. It's easy to glaze over the familiar words and make sure our boxes are checked (or left unchecked, in this case): don't murder, don't steal, yada yada. And don't covet your neighbor's spouse or house – well, I thought I was good with that, until special needs took over our home and consumed our schedules and sanity.

After five years of constant high alert, hyper vigilance, and almost zero dates out with my husband, scrolling social media became a minefield for me when I saw beloved friends' posts about going out to dinner, hiking, and vacationing. *Thou shalt not covet your friend's trip to Hawaii, or their trip to Hatcher Pass, or their trip to the coffeehouse.* Zing. You got me.

But God met me right there, in the tub. It was the kind of bathtub I had longed for during our early marriage, in our apartment renting, condo owning, city living days. We had babysitters and dates then, but no tub. And looking back, I had no dire need for the refuge of one, either.

We each have so much to be grateful for. And yet we each long for things others have that we'd almost be willing to give our eyeteeth for.

In this long season, our dates are in-house, on the couch, with good food and a movie. It's what we need for now – to be home together.

Someday it'll be different and we might need something else. But for now, we are thrilled with this kind of time.

And I've learned to look forward to a certain space at the end of every day. Some quiet, and some books – sometimes a mug of decaf – and a little time to just settle. To reset. To hear my own thoughts. But it could be the bath, or the library, or the mountain, it doesn't matter. It's the space, not the place, because what makes it special is the atmosphere of rest and refilling. Because when we abide, He brings that atmosphere with Him, wherever we are. Whatever we're doing. No matter what time it is. No matter how many things we still have to do.

So friends, show off your dinner plates and oceanside photos all you want, there's no shame. I'm thrilled for you, too.

Because if the antidote to coveting is gratitude (and I'm pretty sure it is), it helps when our gratitude can find a space quiet enough to make itself known every once in a while. We can carry that atmosphere with us wherever, whenever, because He's already there. He is always available, and we don't have to wait until the end of the day to find Him.

spotlight on rest

BY CYNTHIA HELLMAN

Last-minute costume adjustments, an extra bobby pin for good measure. The house lights dim, and a thrill ripples through the audience. The quotidian swish of the curtains herald another opening night.

It's a grueling thing, theatre. We pour ourselves into something only to birth it for a moment before it becomes a mere memory. All of that effort is swept into keepsake boxes, stored on the top shelf of our hearts, and dusted off for reminiscing with the cast.

Ask any actor whether it was worth the stress and effort, the late nights and grief, and the majority will answer with a resounding, "YES!" We aren't gluttons for sorrow and sleep deprivation; we've simply experienced the joy found in the process. The frenetic pace and caffeine-induced palpitations don't hold a candle to what we gain through the pursuit of something beautiful.

I've learned to embrace the frenzy. The urgency doesn't imply chaos; rather, the mechanisms of the show fit together like gears on a clock (most of the time...sometimes stoves fall off the set...but I digress).

In all the busyness of opening night, my favorite moments are before anyone sets foot on the stage. We huddle together backstage, nerves crackle, and Jesus shows up. Because He always does. We lift our voices in praise to Him, and we give the show over to God, the ultimate Creator of beauty, light, and artistry. We pause in the midst of all the hubbub and sit in His presence. We rest in the running.

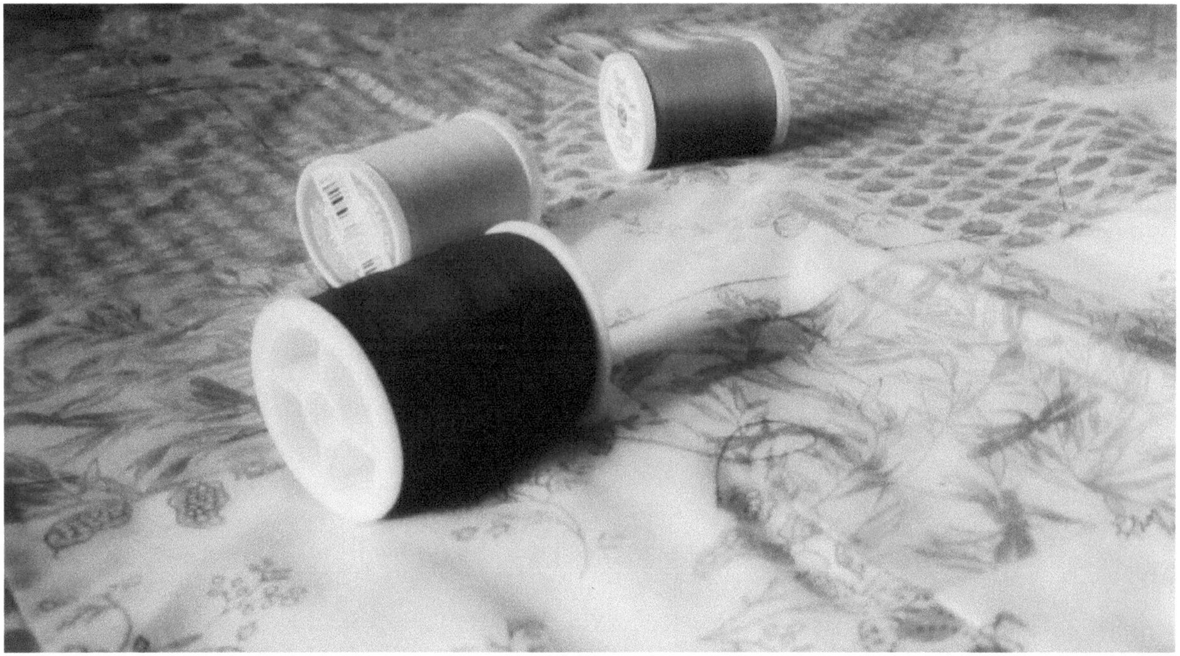

I've learned a great deal from theatre. I know "stage left" from "house left." I've learned cheating[2] is a good thing in theatre, because otherwise the audience stares at your back for the entire show and that's boring and awkward. I've learned how to still my soul before the Host of Heaven no matter what bedlam may be swirling around me. Rest, *true rest* is not dependent on the environment. *True rest* is an outward demonstration of an inward obedience.

I'm reminded of Susanna Wesley, the mother of John and Charles Wesley (along with their seventeen siblings, nine of whom died in infancy). Facing insurmountable challenges and heartbreak on a regular basis, Susanna felt strongly about prayer. With a passel of children underfoot, prayer becomes a challenging feat for me. Not so for Susanna. Her children knew if their mother was perched with her apron over her head, she was not to be disturbed.

In that makeshift meeting tent, Susanna met the Lord in prayer. What was once mundane became sacred in the wake of her stark determination. Ten children kept themselves occupied. Ten pairs of eyes witnessed a hushed holiness descend on their household when their mother's apron draped over her face. And God met her there. Susanna prioritized restfulness in the running of her home and schooling of her children, and taming of her fears, and, and, and...

It's far too easy for me to throw my hands up in mock despair and declare to the God of the universe, "I can't! It's too hard. I'm not ready. I don't have time." In my running, I've forgotten who remains by my side. I've forgotten how to abide in Him despite the busyness. I'm spinning my wheels while He waits for my heart to yield.

As the spotlight dazzles against the velvet curtain, I'm reminded of something I tell my theatre students every time the going gets tough: Dig down deep, draw from every reserve. Then throw your hands up and ask God to take it from there. Because that's where the glory resides, right? It's not in what I can accomplish on my own, but rather in what God accomplishes when my frailty proves too great for the task.

Rest in the running looks like hands up in surrender; it looks like aprons over heads. It looks like you and I bending our souls to Jesus whenever and however we can. There's no formula – only faith.

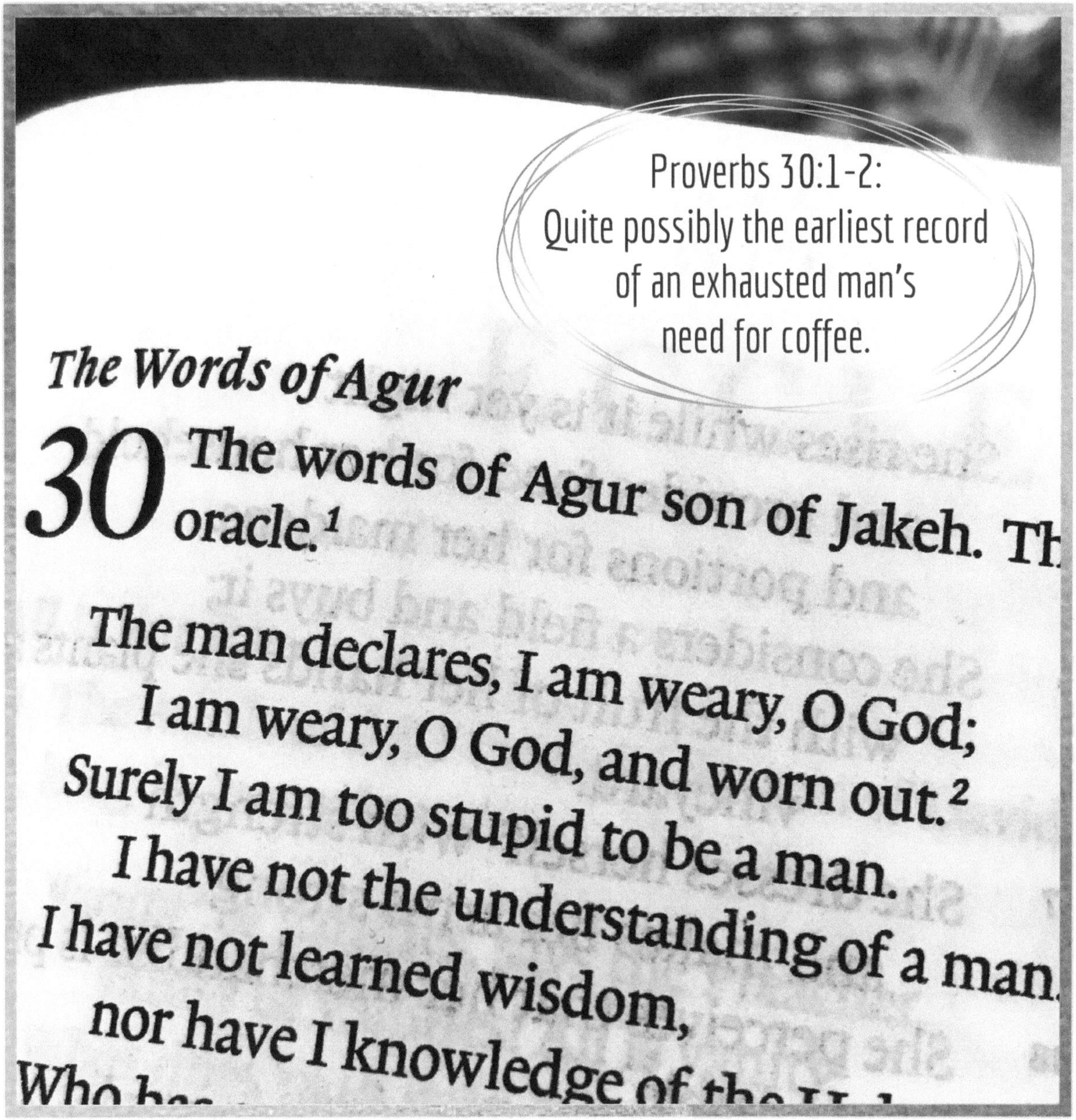
Proverbs 30:1-2:
Quite possibly the earliest record
of an exhausted man's
need for coffee.
The Words of Agur
30 The words of Agur son of Jakeh.
oracle.1
The man declares, I am weary, O God;
I am weary, O God, and worn out.2
Surely I am too stupid to be a man.
I have not the understanding of a man.
I have not learned wisdom,
nor have I knowledge of the

slow fast

It was minus 22 and dark as pitch, and neither of our vehicles started until a friend came by to jump them. Frost covered the bottom of most of our windows. The kids hadn't been outside in daaaays and you could hear it as they played in the evenings, way too loud and restless.

And it wasn't just them, because we had kittens, too – in jaunty audacity, one of them shot right across my laptop, and in one swift move she scrolled the screen, adjusted the volume, and opened a pop-up that asked if I wanted to translate the page to English.

Great. I thought it *was* in English.

She had no proper reverence for the keyboard and raced across it just like everything else, until a hush would fall and she'd cuddle in my lap. And she was so sweet, I could almost forgive her for peeing in the bookshelf right behind my stack of Dickens works.

The cold snap, for us and many friends, lined up with a season of fasting and prayer. And it was perfect: slowing down, checking for drafts, keeping warm by doing less but making sure you're doing the important things. Making sure we're not leaking energy to the wrong places, and asking God for His alignment. Being more creative with the limits around us, and seeing possibilities we never would've considered in the warm comfort zone of our normal routines.

The confinement and cold are temporary. The fasting is temporary. The prayer is not. And the changes He brings in this season are long lasting and life giving, worth every bit of frost and restlessness as we seek Him in the dark.

We can move slower to get more done, but that only happens through action that follows abiding. The rest before the rushing begets a deliberate productivity that my frenzy can't come close to.

We move a little slower, similar to the way fasting shuts down certain functions so the body can focus more on what really needs purified. But much is happening under the surface that we don't see. Sin, distractions, and other toxins are pulled out to make room for growth, healing, and victory.

It's more than decluttering the house or the calendar; it's clearing out the mental, emotional, and spiritual interference so life and its routines are streamlined to align with His mission for our family. We're taking time for determined calculations. The days are crucial, the times are momentous, and we must leverage the hours, information, and opportunities He's given us.

One specific way He has me doing that is by carefully choosing what to read. In the limited hours I have with that longed-for cup of tea and a book after the kids are in bed, that usually means passing on fluffy modern fiction to read classics. I tend to be a slow reader, and classics almost always guarantee time well spent.

Our continued education matters more than ever in this time He has placed us in; how He uses us in the future will have much to do with how we prepare ourselves now. What will we fill ourselves with in the waiting and resting, as we seek Him in the dark?

Complex characters with choices and consequences matter. Vocabulary and great writing matter. Moral integrity matters – and even in books whose main character is like Scarlett O'Hara, they contain genuine struggle, deep relationships, and ethical repercussions that reflect truth in the aftermath.

> *"All things are lawful," but not all things are helpful. "All things are lawful," but not all things build up.*
>
> *– 1 Corinthians 10:23*

Just as we grow best outside our comfort zone, we learn more when we push ourselves a little. I've learned that I'm far more articulate when I'm in the middle of several classics. Just ask Vince – may God help the husband who tries to debate his wife when she's been on a Jane Austen reading spree.

Even on a cold day when the high is seven below zero, there's not enough time or tea in the world to read all the books I want to. But much is still happening under the surface in these slow, steady steps of obedience. As we rest intentionally, God teaches us to handle new conditions (like the abundance of information, misinformation, and social media) with traditional values (like truth, discernment, and courtesy).

> *[T]he lessons of great men are lost unless they re-enforce upon our minds the highest demands which we make upon ourselves; they are lost unless they drive our sluggish wills forward in the direction of their highest ideals.*
> *- Jane Addams, 1903 address in honor of George Washington*

We're learning to approach modern chaos with old simplicity. We are a work in progress. He is doing the work as we trust Him – bringing peace to our homes and hearts, fruition to our dreams and goals, and wisdom for what He is calling us to and moving us toward.

We can trust Him for words and leading, and He will bring light, warmth, and color to dark, cold places as we partner with Him.

He will bring healing to brokenness.

He will bring holy brokenness to pride and mockery.

He will bring joy and comfort to the grieving.

The cold never lasts forever. And neither does fasting, and neither does a metaphorical valley. Warm weather has its own kind of beautiful, but we don't get a view like this without the hardship of cold. Similarly, we only develop certain strengths through the forced, deliberate rest of fasting.

There's peace for this season, and fruit and warmth at the end of it. It's worth our time to abide, and listen, and obey, and use the words He gives us. The coming days will be different because we prayed and obeyed in these ones.

stopping by woods on a snowy evening

BY ROBERT FROST, 1923

Whose woods these are I think I know.
His house is in the village though;
He will not see me stopping here
To watch his woods fill up with snow.

My little horse must think it queer
To stop without a farmhouse near
Between the woods and frozen lake
The darkest evening of the year.

He gives his harness bells a shake
To ask if there is some mistake.
The only other sound's the sweep
Of easy wind and downy flake.

The woods are lovely, dark and deep,
But I have promises to keep,
And miles to go before I sleep,
And miles to go before I sleep.

peacemaker

Calm. White space. Quiet.

We tend to think of peace as the opposite of conflict and noise, but peace is not the presence of only sunshine and rainbows. *Peace* is His presence in the middle of the storm that threatens to destroy your shelter.

We have access to peace because He is with us. In the midst of conflict, we grasp His presence as our shelter, and that is peacemaking.

> *Blessed are the peacemakers, for they shall be called sons of God. Blessed are those who are persecuted for righteousness' sake, for theirs is the kingdom of heaven.*
> *– Matthew* 5:9-10

Peacemakers are not those who live in sterile ease, away from the chaos and mess of life. Peacemaking can only be done in the middle of conflict.

Peacemaking is not busybody activity, butting into people's business and telling them how to get along. Peacemaking is also not a passive, superficial tolerance of others.

Peacemaking is not something we contrive, conjure, or emanate as we yank ourselves up by our bootstraps.

We step into the conflict He calls us to – the hard mission, the difficult relationship, the risky endeavor — and we are not alone in the persecution. He is right here with us.

In the middle of the night, with three sick children and no time to sleep.

In the middle of a family dinner, in the awkward silence that follows heated disagreement.

In the middle of a war zone, running to rescue while dodging crossfire.

We can be in the middle of chaos – screaming children, angry people, dangerous situations – and be so secure in His presence that we remain unruffled. We can be a person of maturity

who gives grace to others instead of defaulting to offense and outrage. It's all His doing, but we do get better at it with practice.

> *Let love be genuine.*
> *Abhor what is evil;*
> *hold fast to what is good.*
> *Love one another with brotherly affection.*
> *Outdo one another in showing honor.*
> *Do not be slothful in zeal,*
> *Be fervent in spirit,*
> *Serve the Lord.*
> *Rejoice in hope,*
> *Be patient in tribulation,*
> *Be constant in prayer.*
> *- Romans 12:9-12*

So in the conflict, or the unknowing, or the dread over what's to come, we can hold peace with two hands because He is wisdom for us, He is security for us, and He is our shelter and protection.

And then He gives us that peace as a weapon to wield against the enemy and all his conniving schemes. Because we weren't just meant to rest in peace; we're meant to be conquer darkness with it, too.

Peacemaking is taking His presence as a shield in the midst of the conflict He calls us to, and drawing others into its shelter. It is the cleanup operation that gives us His wisdom, perspective, strength, and solution in the middle of the struggle.

He is God-With-Us, His kids. We lean into His strength and wield it for His kingdom.

hot water

I turned on the water for Reagan and left the room while she got ready for the shower – which, of course, meant draping every article of clothing on the floor like a hopscotch of small bath mats – and by the time I came back, she was pulling the curtain aside to step in.

Steam poured out of the shower, and still she went forward. I touched the water just in time and stopped her.

"Reagan, is the water the right temperature?"

"Um, yes?" she answered, but her look was confused. I asked her to feel it, and she pulled her hand back immediately.

"Do you want to take a shower in that, or is it too hot?"

"It's too hot?" She wasn't really asking; most of her statements just inflect that way. And *not* asking is often the problem – she often does things without asking first if she should. But it's not usually on purpose and it's not her fault; she didn't choose to be born with Fetal Alcohol Syndrome and all the damage it comes with. This wouldn't be the first time she stepped in something too hot for her.

I've done the same thing, though.

Just the other day, I was not feeling well and was far too exhausted to carry on a conversation with any standard of lucidity. But I needed to arrange coverage for something at church and time was running short, so I recklessly plunged forward and dialed anyway. The person didn't answer, but her voicemail did, and I left the most ridiculous, incoherent string of sentences you ever heard, topping it all off with bungling my own phone number. Awesome.

And yet somehow a few hours later, I was able to glance at the coupon on the fridge for a free massage, go to the bathroom, come back, and still remember the number of the massage therapist and leave a rational message. It might be a reflection of my priorities, or it might be because this time I learned from my mistake. Because this time, I prayed first: *Please God, help me not sound like an idiot.*

I think it's one of those prayers that He loves to answer, because the effectiveness of our ministry to others depends on whether or not we first allow God to minister to us. We have a hard time reflecting Him when we're so busy pushing forward with our own agenda that we forget to be in His presence and make sure that our agenda and timing is in alignment with His.

We learned years ago – maybe you did, too – that if we are going to be effective, nurturing parents (read: loving, patient, wise, and so on) we first need to be effective, nurturing spouses.

Taking care of our marriage comes before taking care of our kids, because it is the oxygen mask that allows us to breathe while making sure everyone else has what they need. Too many families like ours aren't making it, and sacrificing our marriage on the altar of adoptive, special needs parenting doesn't do the Kingdom (or our biological kids, or our adopted kids) any favors.

We prioritize our marriage over our parenting because it is the healthiest way to care for our kids as we first care for our relationship with our spouse. In the same way, we prioritize our relationship with God – by hearing Him, talking to Him, and being in His presence – before our ministry in serving Him. Without it, our ministry is a hollow shell of works without substance.

> *His presence is fire. Without it, no light. Our imitation of Him is only a puff of hot air if we aren't actually spending time with Him.*
> *- Oh My Soul* [3]

We can only fake it for so long before the hot air bursts through thin spots in our shell, and the shrapnel of it flies everywhere.

For us, part of this means that during Communion or any other part of the worship service, I need to be open to hearing God's word for me, instead of only (or even primarily) interceding for others to hear His words for them. I need to get my own oxygen mask on first so I don't pass out while trying to help someone else. My priorities must be aligned for my ministry to be effective.

It also means that our church culture needs to allow room for margin and rest and refilling. Our pastors need time to not minister so they can be filled. Our teachers and other volunteers need to be able to attend services and not just serve all day on Sundays. Our prayer ministers also need to be prayed for. Our leaders who counsel others in crisis and trauma also need counseling and ministry for the high levels of responsibility in their own lives.

I have been guilty of pushing too far on empty, pressing too hard on my own agenda, or even leaning too hard into the good things that are God's agenda, but doing them in an off-balanced way. And the pressure, left unchecked by His presence, explodes through our weak spots and leaves us and those we love bleeding.

We have to ask first: Is *this the right thing, or the right time for it? Is this too much? Am I in Your presence enough to hear You?*

Am I willing to hear You give me the answer I don't want to hear?

Is this water too hot?

What this *doesn't* mean is that our churches should create a culture that enables weak, easy, or shallow Christianity.

> *Sometimes the very advantages of a given geographic setting can make it unnecessary for the people indigenous in that setting to have to develop their human capital to the fullest.*
> - Thomas Sowell, Basic Economics[4]

If we are spoiled with easy living in a land that simply produces everything we need, we won't develop the grit, knowledge, and sense of urgency necessary to survive harsher seasons and climates. We still need to be able to do hard things and learn steadfastness in the struggle, in the same way that those of us raising our kids in Christian homes don't want our kids to take their upbringing for granted. Life throws plenty of punches and we need to grow, mature, and become strong enough to handle whatever comes.

But our desire to build strength and grow is no excuse for neglect or recklessly exposing our kids, family, or church body to harm. We teach our children life skills and safety measures; we must also teach our churches boundaries, awareness, and maturity so we don't unintentionally bring further harm to those who are already walking wounded.

The thing is, we wouldn't know we needed these skills if we hadn't already experienced the consequences of not having them.

We wouldn't know how diligent we need to be in our parenting if we had less kids, or easier kids. Those Pinterest-perfect households might think they've got this parenting thing nailed, but we live over here at the Lighthouse with eight kids and at least as many special needs, and it often feels like we're living out the Parenting X Games. We know how hard it gets, how mistakes can cost us, and how desperately we need God's help and wisdom.

We are stronger only because we know how weak we are without Him.

We wouldn't know our marriage needed nurturing if it were always easy. It took falling apart seven years into it to realize that we needed to make serious changes in how we communicate and connect with each other. But the harsh climate of that season taught us how to take the heat, and we are stronger for it. Now we know to check our oxygen masks, asking each other daily in a dozen different ways: *How are you doing? How is your heart, what are you dreaming about, how is your thought life?*

Is *the water too hot?*

Maybe we need to be better at asking our friends that, too.

He's never told us we have to jump in the hot water – He gave us the tools to change the temperature. He also teaches us how to heal our own burns, and to take care of the wounded. The same Church that is a sanctuary is also the emergency room, and we're called to be a teaching hospital.

Getting burned from stepping into hot water doesn't have to be the end. Sometimes it's the beginning – the lesson we need to start over, equipped with the grit, knowledge, and skills we need to thrive in any climate He puts us in.

how to find breath when you are drowning

BY NATASHA METZLER

Every month the list got longer.

I wanted a baby so desperately and when the years of infertility started marking up my life with sorrow and loss and sadness — I was determined to do everything within my power to change it.

My diet. My doctor. My daily life.

Each month I worked at more, hoping to see the one change I wanted most of all: a pregnancy.

But despite my most determined self-effort, what I longed for most stayed just out of my grasp. Like I was running a race and the finish line kept moving further and further ahead the faster I ran.

I was out of breath and out of hope and out of faith.

Psalm 46:10 says, “Be still, and know that I am God.” And I dutifully added this instruction to my to-do list. *Sit quiet*, I would tell myself, *and pay attention to who God is.* Maybe this would be the key to fixing my body and my dreams and my everything?

But then one day I started studying the Hebrew word that is translated here as “be still.” It’s a verb that has nothing to do with being quiet and everything to do with relaxing and letting go. In fact, one of the definitions is the word “sink,” like you’re grasping onto a mangled broken board in the middle of the ocean trying to keep from drowning and God is whispering, “Let go, dear one; allow yourself to sink and you’ll know that I’m God.”

At first glance it feels crazy. You can’t let go! You’ll die. If you sink below the water, you’ll never be able to catch your breath.

Yet, there is a promise mixed with this instruction. A calling to trust.

Relax, the Father says. *Rest. Stop striving. Stop fighting. Let go. I am God and I am everything you need.*

I had to pry my fingers off that board — the endless lists of things to do to fix my barrenness — and force my own surrender. It really did feel like drowning. Like I was gasping for breath and catching mouthfuls of water instead.

I stood beside my husband one day and sobbed out the agony of letting go of my determination to fight infertility with all my time and money and attention — and accepted that I was not the one who could save myself. Either God would change this for me, or it would remain unchanged. But did I believe that He was everything He said He was? That He would be enough, that He would be God — even if I never bore a child?

Be still, and know that I am God.

Wait, child, and know that I am God.

Sink, my daughter, and as the waves crash — know that I am God.

At one point during my infertility journey, the thought of five years without a baby nearly broke me — but I faced the very thing I feared the most and I survived. Not just survived, but I discovered that the goodness of God is available in the most barren of places. He did everything He said He would, and I walked through more and more years until over a decade of barrenness was behind me.

Over a decade of facing my worst fear became over a decade of knowing God in a deep, abiding, brilliant way. I discovered joy and hope and more faith than I could have imagined.

Letting go, sinking, waiting — being still — didn't leave me drowned. Instead, God gave me hope and life and breath.

Wherever you are, friend, know this truth: God is exactly who He says He is.

And when He tells you to let go, He'll always be there, arms outstretched. You might choke, you might cry, you might hurt — but you'll breathe. You'll survive. Because He is enough.

Always, always enough.

on rough days

February started all silver and white that morning. Ten degrees, and all the chimneys across the valley were slowly puffing their smoke toward the west while we drank our morning coffee.

I was on the couch next to Vince, listening to him try to get through to customer service as he took care of some bills. They transferred him to a "press 1 for this, press 2 for that" menu and he was caught in a loop - no matter what he pressed, it sent him back to the same place.

Somehow he found another route that asked him to speak instead of enter his request, and after saying "CUSTOMER SERVICE" first in a normal voice and then again, just for fun, like P.T. Barnum – both of which were ineffective – he started in on a particular children's worship song that gave me a sudden desire to stab him with a pen.

"Sorry," he said, "I'm just trying to get through this."

"Yeah, me too," I said, "but if you keep singing that, you won't make it."

So began Monday.

And here's a good word for those of us in the middle of a rough day – if we are walking through hardship or conflict, or willful misunderstanding, or hope deferred, or disaster and heartache, or we're just simply irritated by loved ones before our coffee has kicked in:

> *Let them thank the Lord for His steadfast love,*
> *For His wondrous works to the children of man.*
> *For He satisfies the longing soul,*
> *And the hungry soul He fills with good things.*
> - *Psalm* 107:8-9

No matter what it looks like, He's still doing. He is still satisfying the longing soul. He is still filling the hungry soul with good things. He is still doing wondrous works for His people.

On one of those rough days, I spent hours underneath a sick preschooler and his 103 temperature. He puked all over my bed before his fever finally broke, and once we got it cleaned up, we thought we were in the clear. But no, my friends, we were *not* in the clear, because an hour later he was violently shoving away the bucket I held for him, somehow managing to puke all over himself *and* the only part of the couch that was not already covered in towels.

Did I mention that day started with the geriatric cat vomiting into my hands as I tried to protect a different surface? No? Well, that happened, too. So gross.

That day, I also got to schedule fun appointments like a CT scan and physicals (because, Dorothy, we're not in our thirties anymore) and I was looking at paperwork for a neurologist that I had already decided to put off until the following morning. Ain't nobody got time for that on a day like this one.

Some days we're just out of words. We're praying without ceasing and loving the hurting and watching for good news because we know it's here somewhere – even in sickness, even in grief, even when we know we're walking into pain because He calls us off the couch and out of our comfort zone and into the mess. He is unchanging. He's still the Good News, and He's still right here with us.

It is okay to pray without words because He promises that He has words for us.

> *Likewise the Spirit helps us in our weakness. For we do not know what to pray for as we ought, but the Spirit himself intercedes for us with groanings too deep for words. And he who searches hearts knows what is the mind of the Spirit, because the Spirit intercedes for the saints according to the will of God.*
> - *Romans 8:26-27*

If it came down to us having to pray with the right words, then we've made it about what we can fix or do or achieve, instead of what He does for us and how much we need Him. And if it's about what we do for ourselves, then we get the glory instead of Him – and He knows we can't handle the weight of that.

Some days we end strong. But at the end of other days I am asking God, Did I do enough? And He responds, Is *it about you doing enough, or is it about what I'm doing*? And then He reminds me that trusting Him is also something we do.

At the end of the day, we can stop our striving and fretting. At the end of the week, we can let go of the things that did not get done. Write them down if you need to, and let go of them for the night. God is on the night shift, not sleeping, always working the weekends, ever on our side, watching over all the details that are trying to keep us from peace and joy. Rest makes for a more productive tomorrow.

Even when all the intangibles look unfinished and not progressing, trusting Him while abiding does a great work – and it positions us for breakthrough, more than any doing or striving ever will.

deep sigh

BY RENEE PETTY

Deep sigh: an exhalation of breath I didn't know I was holding. This is often the external indicator of my internal striving and weariness of soul. At 41 years old, my entire family recognizes this as a sign that I am tired. Not I *didn't get sleep* tired, but deep down in my bones tired. This year, these past few years. I've done a lot of sighing.

It's been a season full of loss, change, uncertainty and heartache. Seasons like this often tempt me into *pull yourself up by your bootstraps and plow ahead* mode. After all, self reliance is an Alaskan badge of honor; we wear it well, and it always produces striving.

{deep sigh}

> *Then Jesus said, "**Come to me**, all of you who are weary and carry heavy burdens, and I will give you rest."*
> *- Matthew* 11:28

Come to me – an invitation, open ended, always extended. The rest God offers isn't the "put your feet up and zone out to Netflix" kind of rest. His rest is more like a trade; we give Him our troubles, our fears, our doubts, and in return He provides the peace our souls need.

The rest is in the invitation, **Come to me**, for true rest is found not in holding still, but in drawing near to God. The soul reaching, bone deep rest we long for is found in proximity to Jesus and nowhere else. Jesus knows what exhaustion feels like, and he understands our weariness for he too experienced it here on earth. He is ready, waiting even, to give what you are needing in days of ceaseless running. *You just have to ask, to draw near.* Hebrews 4:16 instructs us, *Let us then with confidence draw near to the throne of grace, that we may receive mercy and find grace to help in time of need.* Or, for us more stubborn, boot-strap pulling believers (aka, Alaskans), the Message says it this way – *So let's walk right up to him and get what he is so ready to give. Take the mercy, **accept the help.***

Accept the help, stop striving and pressing, stop numbing and chilling. Lay all of it before the throne of Jesus, draw near to the One who understands even more than we could. Here you will find wisdom, understanding, peace and rest, and the strength to move forward or stand still. Here you can stop holding your breath. Here you can let out the pain, confusion, and tumult, and inhale the very presence of the living God. Breathe deep, friends.

better than it looks

Over the weekend we watched *Gone with the Wind* with our kids, who had never seen it before. So picture this: We're at the scene where Scarlett and Ashley are in the field after the war is over, and she tempts him to run away with her, and Ashley almost gives in but steels himself. Remember this part?

He tells Scarlett, "There's one thing on this earth that you love more than me – Tara." And he scoops up a handful of dirt from the ground and presses it into her hand.

The dramatic silence in the room is suddenly broken by an incredulous question from our nine-year-old.

"Did he just give her *horse poop*?"

Uh, no. But yeah, I guess it sorta looked like it. Sometimes it takes a kid to point this stuff out.

We explained that it was dirt; he gave her land. Ashley reminded Scarlett of her inheritance. *Ohhh*, she said, sort of understanding, but not really. She'll understand more when she's older.

But I had my own epiphany around that weekend. We had been filming a study and I was still terribly uncomfortable in front of the camera; my brain seemed to shut down whenever I sat in front of it and I couldn't remember more than a sentence at a time of what I was supposed to be saying. So far we'd spent five weeks wrestling with my printed notes – trying to enlarge them, trying to hang them off the camera with any number of engineering fails involving rubber bands, clothespins, and paperclips to keep them from spinning away at an angle I couldn't see.

We spent more time trying to get the notes to hold still than actual filming. And then I ran out of printer ink, and we were in real trouble.

If only we had a screen, I thought. *A screen where we could enlarge the font...and then just scroll as needed to the next section...almost like...*

OH. MY. WORD.

Almost like the screen of the laptop.

You know, where I wrote all the content in the first place.

After that discovery, things sped right along but it was still a huge leap outside the comfort zone. I learned that it doesn't matter how well you normally speak English, because once the camera is rolling you somehow transform into a drunken-sounding idiot with a whole new vacubulary. I mean, vabocularу. Err, bovaculary. Whatever. It's nothing that 47 retakes couldn't take care of.

But this theme of things not being as bad as we think kept coming up. Sometimes a situation seems terrible – no ink in the printer when you need it is bad, yes? – but that very problem often leads us to a solution staring us in the face, just waiting to be recognized.

Earlier that month we fought fear for over a week, waiting for news about a health concern that would have affected generations in our family. The follow up appointment finally came and revealed that all systems were go – it was all good news, the enemy was lying and fear mongering, and things were, as is usually the case, better than they looked.

If we can preach this to ourselves, it will help keep our minds and spirits at rest: Usually things are better than they seem, and working out to something better than we could have imagined.

> *I want you to know, brothers, that* ***what has happened to me has really served to advance the gospel,*** *so that it has become known throughout the whole imperial guard and to all the rest that my imprisonment is for Christ. And most of the brothers, having become confident in the Lord by my imprisonment, are much more bold to speak the word without fear.*
> *- Philippians 1:12-14*

We think life is handing us horse poop, but no, not always. Usually it is God, giving us land – reminding us of our inheritance, and telling us to fight for it.

> *I do not cease to give thanks for you, remembering you in my prayers, that the God of our Lord Jesus Christ, the Father of glory, may give you the Spirit of wisdom and of revelation in the knowledge of him, having the eyes of your hearts enlightened,* ***that you may know what is the hope to which he has called you,*** *what are the riches of his glorious inheritance in the saints.*
> *- Ephesians 1:16-18*

He tells us how to see what is right in front of us, because without His vision our understanding is limited. We don't see the solution because we're focused on the problem.

But when we focus on our inheritance – the hope to which He has called us, with our understanding enlightened, surrendered to receive His wisdom and revelation – we fight for our territory and expand it. We know it's ours, regardless of how bad things look.

> *There is something very thrilling about standing in a place of shelter while a gale roars by over your head. One tastes the excitement of violence without the fear.*
> *- Elizabeth Goudge* [5]

We go from fighting fear and uncertainty to standing in ridiculous peace, even while we still don't exactly know what's ahead.

And, do we ever really know what's ahead, anyway? No.

Accepting that is what positions us for peace in the unknowing. He holds us no matter what things look like, wherever we go.

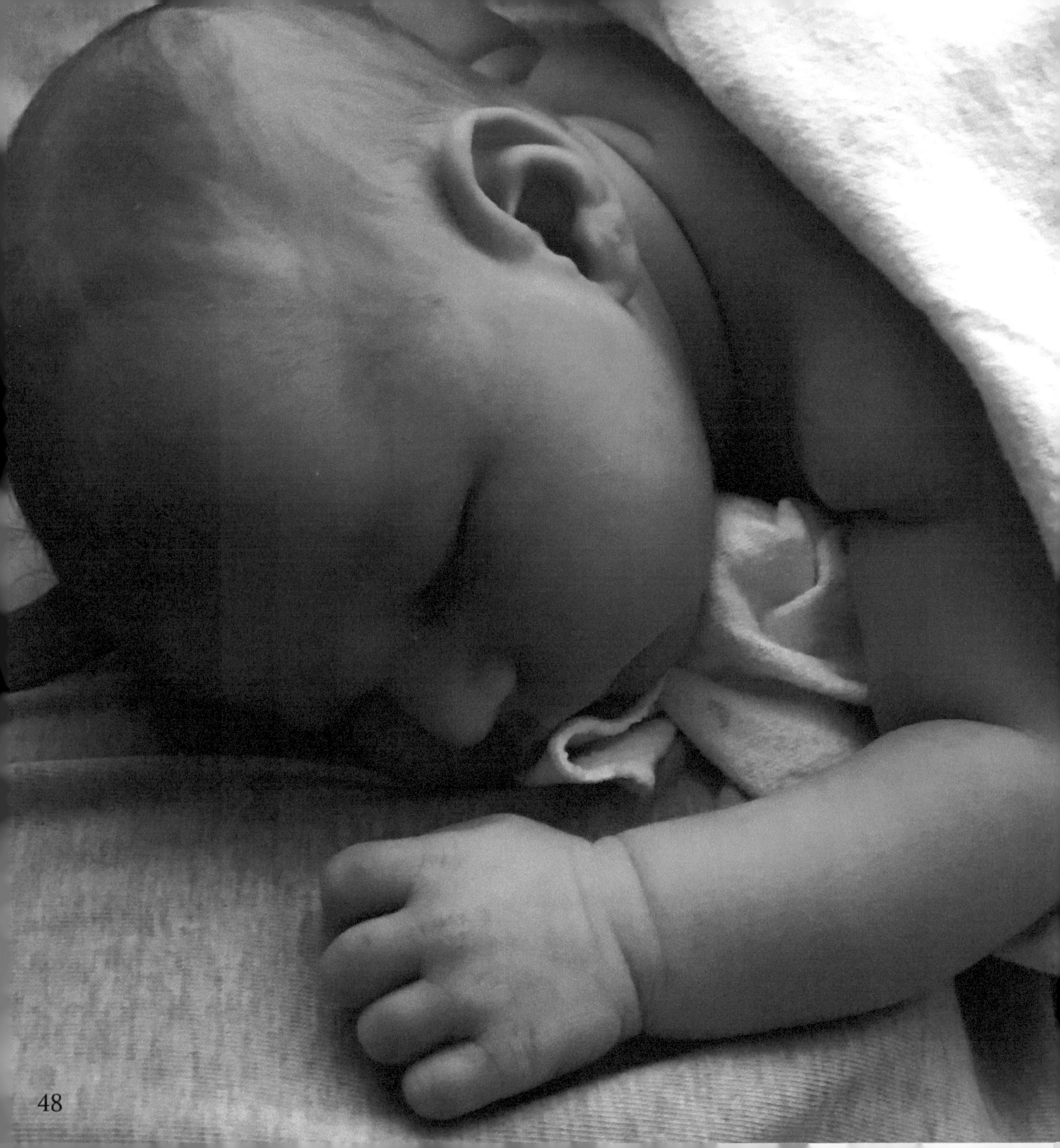

Everyone loves to hold
the sleeping baby.
God loves and longs
to hold us, too,
when we are at rest,
with all our weight
on Him.

valentine epiphany

BY JESSICA DASSOW

I'm concerned I'm turning into one of those moms who hate Valentine boxes.

I've always loved that sort of festive preparation, so this throws me for a bit of a loop. This attitude has come about slowly, though it feels sudden. Life has become so bursting at the seams there's just no time left for...well, for anything other than keeping our heads above water. Burning it at both ends has become the norm.

It used to be, for many years, that my husband and I would do the "suppertime crazy" followed by the "bedtime crazy," and then, with little people snug in their beds, we would fall into exhausted heaps on the couch to have some talk time or play a little cards or watch a movie or make a snack. Some of this has not changed. We still do suppertime crazy followed by bedtime crazy, but now we have teenagers. They plop down on the couches next to us after the littlest people are put to bed, but unlike us, they are not exhausted. They are invigorated and ready to talk about life and projects and feelings and dreams...and we LOVE that they want to talk about these things with us. Except, we are exhausted.

When we finally bow out from the wonderful conversation because our eyelids won't stay open, it is way too late again and we fall into bed. The alarm goes off in about ten minutes (swear!) and we do it all over again. The potty training toddler. Forever and always meal and snack prep and cleanup. Algebra. Research on bats and birds. Persuasive essays. Teaching cursive letters. Chemistry. College applications. Job applications. Violin practice. Occupational therapy appointments. Dentist appointments.

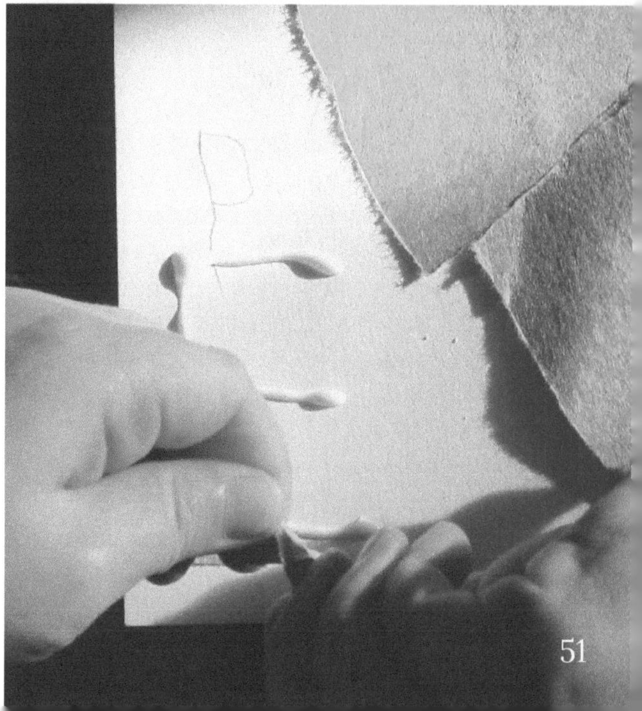

So, that is why, when glue sticks and construction paper and kleenex boxes and googled images of Valentine box ideas invaded the already-stacked-foot-high-with-homeschool-books-and-leftover-lunch table, this mom began to crack today. Deeply desiring to encourage the fun and creativity, I smiled and started a little pot of espresso. Surely that would help me get in the spirit for the upcoming holiday, right? As I swirled whipped cream on my mocha and just sat down to fuel up for the upcoming task, a chorus of creative-genius-gone-tragic piped up from the table.

"I want to make a mailbox, too!"

"Well, you can't. Make something else."

"A military tank is too hard!"

"My glue stick is running out!"

"Where's the tape?!"

An hour and a stone cold coffee later, we had three Valentine box creations stashed in my closet for safekeeping until the big day...along with a mom who realized she's starting to be a mom who hates Valentine boxes.

So with my heated up mocha in hand, I'm thinking this through. Because you see, I don't want to be a mom who hates Valentine boxes. I want to be a fun mom. A spontaneously adventurous mom. A creative mom. I want to be more like the mom I used to be before I began to feel so overwhelmed with the demands of life and responsibilities and expectations. I can blame it all on the upheaval we've been through in the last four and a half years, which includes four moves, two job changes, and a new baby. But in my heart I know that's a cop-out. Somehow, there had to have been subtle changes of thought and perspective that led to this feeling of overwhelm.

Somehow I have succumbed to believing I have to "do it all," and do it all seemingly perfect. The reality? It just ain't happenin'. "Perfect" is a lie. What's true is that life is full. Life is a big, fat mess. And it's also so, so beautiful if I just remember that I can breathe and live and abide in the grace upon grace that He so freely gives. My job is just to abide. To point to Him. To be okay with things being chaotic and full and imperfect during this season.

Things won't always look this way. Things will be a little different tomorrow. And next week. And definitely in a month from now, and oh-so-different a year from now. What a tragedy it will be if I don't live this fully and enjoy what is now. Kids are quickly growing and on the verge of flying. It will be quiet. It will be less mess and noise. And I will miss it all. Even the Valentine boxes.

A thing of beauty is a joy forever.
A clean stovetop of white is a joy for three minutes.

homemade queso

But homemade queso is a joy until you either run out of it or you run out of stuff to dip in it. My favorite way to eat it is with homemade pretzels, but tortilla chips work just fine. Also, do you *see* those clean areas of the white stovetop?! Those areas, my friends, are the result of careful camera positioning. Thankyouverymuch.

ingredients:
(double or quadruple as necessary)
2 T butter
2 T flour
1/3 cup milk
1 cup shredded cheddar cheese (feel free to substitute and experiment with other cheeses)
Salt, pepper, cayenne and/or chili powder

1 Melt the butter in a pan and stir in the flour to make a roux. Quickly add the milk a little at a time and stir as it thickens.

2 Add the cheddar and stir as it all melts together into cheesy dreaminess. Turn off the heat, and add salt, pepper, and cayenne to taste. If you're adventurous (or just wanting it to seem more like health food), you can also add sautéed mushrooms, sliced green onions, chopped jalapeño peppers, or diced tomatoes.

3 Pour it over rice, or dip chips in it, or talk a culinary-minded family member into making homemade pretzels. Or, stir cooked macaroni noodles into it and violà! You have homemade mac and cheese, and the gratitude of all your family members...if you decide to share.

instant pot chuck roast

BY MĒGAN ANCHETA

makes 4-6 servings

An easy recipe that produces tender and juicy pieces of beef with a rich and flavorful broth. This melt-in-your-mouth roast requires no browning, which cuts down on the prep time significantly. It is a very simple and naturally gluten-free beef recipe, yet the few ingredients needed impart incredible flavor.

ingredients:
3-3.5 lbs. beef chuck roast
1 cup water
1/3 cup full-bodied red wine (such as cabernet sauvignon, or a merlot)
1 1/2 tablespoons gluten-free Worcestershire sauce
1 1/4 teaspoons sea salt
1/2 teaspoon garlic powder
1/2 teaspoon ground black pepper
4-5 sprigs fresh thyme (or 1/2 teaspoon dried)
1 sprig fresh rosemary (or 1/2 teaspoon dried)

1 Pour the water, red wine, and Worcestershire sauce into the stainless steel bowl of the Instant Pot.

2 Add the beef chuck roast and then sprinkle with sea salt, garlic powder, and ground black pepper.

3 Place the fresh thyme and rosemary sprigs on top of the roast, and then click the lid into place on the Instant Pot. Set the vent to seal.

4 Cook for 115 minutes (1 hour and 55 minutes) at high pressure. When the Instant Pot is done cooking, it will come down from pressure naturally, about 28-30 minutes. (I do not recommend using quick release with this recipe. Natural release ensures tender and juicy meat. If you are in a hurry, try to give it at least 15 minutes of natural release before letting out the rest of the pressure manually.)

surrendering to rest

Saturdays, as much as I can make them, are about stitches and pages. Quiet thinking, and time to talk about things that normally get blown through in the week. I have too many projects going at once – I know I do, and it's always been that way – but on perfect, nothing-scheduled Saturdays, I can pick my favorite projects to work on, and my favorite books to read, and blissfully ignore the rest.

The book I'm reading that bugs me? Not today. Hiding ends in the blanket I'm working on? Not if I don't want to. Fixing Andrey's slippers with the blown-out toes? Not a chance.

Rest, for some of us, is a hard thing to learn. How are you doing with this? Are you a good rester? Or does rest for you look like only doing half a million things at once, instead of the whole million?

Rest, and how we do it — or whether we do it at all— is a huge part of our identity. It reflects our priorities and it's also part of our obedience. And how we do it (or if we do it at all) reflects our security, whether we walk as His bride or as our own idol.

I'm still a work in progress at this. And we're all different; there's no formula that works for each of us. For example, maybe naps are a great thing for you. But for me, I'll lay down and try to nap, completely exhausted, borderline cranky, staring at the inside of my eyelids for several minutes before I give up, resigned to just lay there awake and bored until the time is up. Apparently in this area at least, I haven't changed since I was a preschooler.

But I'm slowly figuring it out: We are meant to rest, but rest only comes in surrender.

We can't do it when we're striving or trying to control everything. We can't do it when we're partnered with fear or bound by insecurity. We can't do it if we insist on always having our own way. But it's hard to let things go when you're used to doing them.

It's hard to know you could (but not necessarily should) be doing things, making progress, getting ahead, or at least not getting behind.

It's hard to trust the kids with things, trust your spouse with things, and — we might as well be honest — trust God with things.

Because we like doing all the things. We know how to do them a certain way. And what if something is left undone?

God has been teaching me that this is a form of idolatry, thinking that we must be the one to do things. Especially when God tells us to rest, but we are afraid He will drop the ball while we're napping.

I'm learning that He never drops the ball. When He tells us to rest, whether it's just for a sabbath or for a season, we can give Him all the balls, all the spinning plates, all the cogs in our wheelhouse. He will handle them better than we could in our striving and pushing. And He will make us better, too.

It's the difference between being meek versus being overbearing — one is strength under control, the other is strength run wild. Only one of them reveals true strength and continues to grow stronger. The other depletes itself and others. One of them trusts the Father to be faithfully in charge and goes forward even in sleep; the other demands to do everything themselves and falls further behind.

> *But the meek shall inherit the land and delight themselves in abundant peace.*
> *- Psalm 37:11*

We rest when we tithe and trust the Lord for provision, and we rest when we invest more time in prayer than in planning. We rest when we prioritize His presence over our production, and somehow we find that the fruit is bigger and healthier for it. We create things with God when we pray, and every minute in prayer does more than many days of effort and striving.

Rest comes to those who are willing to risk surrender. We trust in Perfect Love, and He casts out fear. And when we awake, we're stronger — and ready to inherit the land He's given us.

And it is my prayer
that your *love* may abound
more and more,
with *knowledge* and all *discernment*,
so that you may approve what is excellent,
and so be pure and blameless
for the day of Christ,
filled with the fruit of righteousness
that comes through Jesus Christ,
to the glory and praise of God.

philippians 1:9-11

study guide

This flexible, light-yoked guide is for you to use on your own or with a small group. We've included questions to use for personal journaling or group discussion, scripture to study, copy down, and memorize, and short prompts for prayer. It's not homework or another thing to add to your list – it's just movement forward and rest for your soul, friends.

upper room people

questions

If this new year is a clean slate, what things do I want to write on it?

How has the Lord shown compassion for me this week?

How is God rearranging me as I abide in Him?

scripture

Isaiah 55:6-9, Acts 1:7-14

prayer

Lord, I want the power, not just the plan. Please show me what that looks like in my life right now, and throughout the year.

what we need for now

questions

How is God meeting my need for rest in this season?

How has God met my need for rest in other seasons?

Have I struggled with jealousy in any area? How can I counter that with gratitude?

scripture

Psalm 85:6-9

prayer

Dear God, show me what I've taken for granted in this season and forgive me for missing it. Please open my eyes to what You've given me so I can take full advantage of Your goodness.

spotlight on rest

questions

What are some specific ways I can meet with the Lord throughout the day in spite of busyness?

What do I need God to accomplish right now that I cannot do on my own?

scripture

Isaiah 32:17-18

prayer

Lord, You are with me even in the busiest parts of my day. Help me to see how your grace covers all of my responsibilities.

slow fast

questions

Where am I leaking energy to the wrong places?

What is God telling me to do about it?

What distractions can I temporarily remove to gain more alignment and a better perspective?

scripture

1 Corinthians 10:23 and 31, Isaiah 58

prayer

Holy Spirit, reveal the things You want me to focus on, and give me strategies to deal with the distractions around me. Give me wisdom to discern between things I should eliminate temporarily, and things I should eliminate permanently.

peacemaker

questions

What storm do I need God's peace in right now?

What does God's presence in the middle of this storm look like?

How do I see Him working in this situation? And how do I see Him working in and through me?

scripture

Matthew 5:9-10, Romans 12:9-12

prayer

Lord, show me how to hold peace with two hands right now. Thank you for providing peace in my heart, and for showing me how to wield it for the Kingdom.

hot water

questions

Where do I need the Lord to minister to me right now, before I minister to others?

Do I need to take a pause somewhere in my life before I push forward with my own agenda?

Is the water too hot in any area of my life? What is God telling me to do about it?

scripture

Psalm 37:5-9

prayer

Dear God, show me where I have stepped too far or too early. Give me wisdom and discernment to know when and how to move forward, and when and how to step back.

how to find breath when you are drowning

questions

What am I hanging on to that I need to let go of and trust God with?

What fears am I struggling with as I consider letting go?

What does letting go of that thing actually look like?

scripture

Psalm 46:10, Ephesians 1:3-14

prayer

Jesus, thank you for ministering to my heart as I let this thing go. Help me to be brave and focused on who You are, and how faithful You always are to me.

on rough days

questions

What am I longing for on rough days?

How is the Lord meeting me in those needs?

In what area do I tend to lean on my own strength? What would it look like to surrender this to God?

scripture

Psalm 107:8-9, Romans 8:26-27

prayer

Dear God, thank you for being with me on my rough days. I know You are near, and that You hear me. Help me represent You well, even on days when I am tempted to misrepresent myself. Thank You for covering me with grace.

deep sigh

questions

How can I tell when I am weary from striving?

What do I need to trade with the Lord right now for His rest?

scripture

Matthew 11:28, Hebrews 4:16

prayer

Jesus, You are so near, even when I forget Your presence is right here with me. Show me what I need to lay down, and teach me to trust You more.

better than it looks

questions

What concerns do I have in this season that might actually be better than they look?

How might I gain inheritance through this situation?

How should I fight for the land God is giving me in this season?

scripture

Ephesians 1:16-18, Philippians 1:12-14

prayer

Lord, help me to focus on the inheritance you have given me. Help me to see these situations with Your eyes. Thank You for holding me, and for holding my loved ones.

valentine epiphany

questions

Do I struggle with feeling like I have to do it all, and do it all perfectly?

Is there any area in my life where I am holding myself to unrealistic expectations? How can I step back from those in a healthy way?

scripture

Philippians 2:14-16, Philippians 3:12-16

prayer

Holy Spirit, help me to discern the right priorities for this season. Thank you for being present with me, and for helping me be present with my family and gracious toward myself.

surrendering to rest

questions

In what ways do I live out strength under control, and in what ways do I live out strength run wild?

Is there an area in my life that I am having a hard time trusting God with? What is He telling me to specifically do about that?

How can I invest more time in prayer than planning?

scripture

Psalm 37:3-11, 29-31

prayer

Lord, help me live self-controlled and Spirit-controlled. I trust You to not drop the ball in my life, and to show me when I need to run and when I need to rest.

1. *He said to them, "It is not for you to know times or seasons that the Father has fixed by his own authority. But you will receive power when the Holy Spirit has come upon you, and you will be my witnesses in Jerusalem and in all Judea and Samaria, and to the end of the earth."* (Acts 1:7-8)

2. "Cheating out" is to angle your body so the audience doesn't just see your profile, even if two actors are in a conversation with each other.

3. Shannon Guerra, *Oh My Soul* (Wasilla, Alaska: Copperlight Wood, 2018), 152.

4. Thomas Sowell, *Basic Economics* (New York: Basic Books, 2015), 547.

5. Elizabeth Goudge, *Green Dolphin Street* (Cutchogue, New York: Buccaneer Books, 1944), 10.

also by shannon guerra

the Work That God Sees series

prayerful motherhood in the midst of the overwhelm

Moms, you pour yourselves out every day. How about some powerful refilling, in small, easy doses?

Short chapters. White space. Deep down hope, and out loud laughter. Because you have what it takes. You are watched over and known by the God who notices every detail, and He meets you in these mundane moments and is breathing them into mighty movement.

Work That God Sees is available as six individual little books, or as a complete, all-in-one edition with the content from all six books (including the snarky recipes, crafty patterns, and questions for personal journaling or small group discussion) plus 25 pages of extra stories, recipes, and lessons you can learn at someone else's expense.

Oh My Soul

encountering God in honest, unconventional (and sometimes messy) prayer

What if there was **one thing** you could do that would always, without fail, make you more **whole** and **healed** and **at peace** than you were the day before...would you do it?

What if, at the same time, that one thing transformed the world around you?

This is what happens when we encounter God, living in His presence, in continual conversation with Him.

We want to hear God better, and to know His will for all the messy, mundane details of our life. But does He still speak to us when we are distracted, grumpy, overwhelmed, and unprepared? How can we have "quiet time" with God when there's no quiet, and no time? Can we really know the will of God and move forward in obedience, in spite of our fears and failures?

And, if we're really honest with Him, will He strike us with lightning? Or will we end up praying with boldness and authenticity like never before?

Available as the original book, companion journal, and 21-day devotional study.

upside down

understanding and supporting attachment in adoptive and foster families

This book gives hope to adoptive and foster families, and the lowdown for those who love them.

Adoptive and foster families working through attachment issues often feel alone, but their communities can intentionally be part of the solution instead of unintentionally being part of the problem. Without that support, adoptive and foster families live in isolation.

Shannon Guerra learned this firsthand after she and her husband adopted two of their children in 2012. She started writing shockingly transparent blog posts about what her family was going through at home, at the doctor's office, and in her heart as a mama.

And then adoptive and foster families started writing back.

Their overwhelming, unanimous theme was, **"This is what I've wanted to tell people for so long. I wish everyone who knows our family could read this."**

This book is the result. In about 100 pages, *Upside Down* provides information and insight that transforms an outsider's assumptions into an insider's powerful perspective. Because adoptive and foster families should never feel alone, and our communities can be equipped to make sure they never feel that way again.

one more thing...

Need a little white space in the chaos?

You are warmly invited to copperlightwood.com, where we're transparent about finding peace in the hard moments and beauty in the mess. I hope you'll hit the subscribe button and poke around all the posts and videos. Just keep in mind that it's a little unpolished here, so watch out for the Legos on the floor.

Bless you, friend,
Shannon Guerra

connect:
parler: shannonguerra
mewe: shannonguerra
gab: shannonguerra
clouthub: shannonguerra
facebook: copperlightwood
instagram: copperlightwood
goodreads: shannonguerra
pinterest: copperlightwood

email:
shannon@copperlightwood.com

CPSIA information can be obtained
at www.ICGtesting.com
Printed in the USA
BVHW051337270121
598817BV00001B/6

* 9 7 8 1 7 3 6 0 8 4 4 2 7 *